Read the dictionary entry.

record a. a music disc
b. an official document about events
c. the best achievement ever
d. what a person has done in the past (attendance, voting, crime, etc.)
e. to preserve in writing, sound, or video

Which meaning of *record* is used in the sentence? Write the letter on the line.

1. Her voting record shows that she cares about the environment. ________
2. The band will record three new songs next week. ________
3. Bob Beamon held the men's long jump record for almost 23 years. ________

Write a paragraph using at least three different meanings of the word *record*.

4. ____

WEEK 8 DAY 1 Daily Language Review

Write the sentences correctly.

1. Jed was feed her dog when he heard a loudly noise.

___

2. The horse, it had getted loose and was ran free.

___

Write the missing interjection.

3. "________!" exclaimed Jed, chasing after the runaway horse.

Well Oh no Bravo

Write the plural of each underlined noun.

4. The sound of the horse's <u>hoof</u> scared the <u>ox</u> and the <u>goose</u>.

___ ___ ___

WEEK 8 DAY 2 Daily Language Review

Write the sentences correctly.

1. Angel and Jorge were pick blackberrys in an huge field.

___

2. Mom said Pick careful to avoid the thorns on the bushs.

___

Write the missing interjection.

3. "________!" yelled Angel when a thorn pricked his thumb.

Whew Good Ouch

Draw a line between the root word and the suffix of the underlined word. Then explain what the word means.

4. Angel felt <u>foolish</u> hurting himself after his mother's warning.

___

Write the sentences correctly.

1. Im study the poem "Paul Reveres Ride" in his English class.

2. Its about Reveres famously 1775 ride to Lexington Massachusetts.

Choose the word that best completes the sentence. Then explain your choice.

3. Paul ____________ his important message while riding his horse.

said shouted squealed spoke

Add punctuation to the sentence.

4. The first line of the poem says Listen, my children, and you shall hear.

Write the sentences correctly.

1. There are many sign of spring has arrive.

2. Have you saw rainbow's in a sky after it rains?

Add a descriptive word in each blank.

3. Amy's ____________ chicken laid a ____________ egg.

Draw a line between the prefix and the root word of the underlined word. Then explain what the word means.

4. Green grass <u>reappears</u> after the snow melts.

Read these signal words.

although	for example	so that
in fact	in other words	similarly
otherwise	besides	after all

Which signal word or words best complete each sentence?

1. ____________________ I like watching sports, I prefer to play.
2. ____________________, I joined a local swim club.
3. I'm also saving my money ____________________ I can buy a good tennis racket.

Write a paragraph using at least three signal words from the box.

4. ____

____

____

____

____

____

WEEK 9 DAY 1 Daily Language Review

Write the sentences correctly.

1. Most people knows that Roosters crow when the sun came up.

____

2. as the sun goes down, horses, goats, and sheeps liked to run and play.

____

Combine the sentences to make one sentence.

3. Fireflies can glow in the dark. They start when the sun sets.

____

Complete this analogy.

4. evening : dusk :: morning : ______________

WEEK 9 DAY 2 Daily Language Review

Write the sentences correctly.

1. Irene had a dog named pixie where she was much youngest.

____

2. Pixie loved playing on the yard, but only when it is warm.

____

Write the missing word.

3. Irene tried every trick, but Pixie ______________ not go out in the snow.

   would can should might

4. Irene covered her patio so Pixie ______________ have a dry place outside.

   should can could must

WEEK 9 DAY 3 Daily Language Review

Write the sentences correctly.

1. I have an oldest brother that was born on February 29 2004.

____

2. From most years, february have only 28 days.

____

Combine the sentences to make one sentence.

3. February 29 happens once every four years. It happens in leap years.

____

Write the missing word.

4. Without leap year, summer ____________ start in July in a hundred years.

must should will would

WEEK 9 DAY 4 Daily Language Review

Write the sentences correctly.

1. Brazil is the larger country which sits in the equator.

____

2. The country are wide enough, to have three time zone's.

____

Write the missing words.

3. Brazil has several major rivers, including the ____________.

Amazon river Amazon River amazon river

Complete this analogy.

4. stream : river :: hill : ____________

Read these related words and their meanings.

predict *verb*
to state that something is likely to happen

prediction *noun*
a statement about what is likely to happen

predictable *adjective*
easy to guess what is likely to happen

Which word best completes each sentence?

1. Sandy's test score was ________________________, since she didn't study at all.
2. Julia can ________________________ the end of any story.
3. Computers have helped make weather ________________________ more accurate.

Write a paragraph using all three related words.

4. ____

____

____

____

____

____

WEEK 10 DAY 1 Daily Language Review

Write the sentences correctly.

1. Have you went to the aquarium in New Orleans Louisiana.

___

2. The acuarium has many sea life that live in the Gulf of Mexico.

___

Use context clues to figure out the meaning of the bold word. Write the meaning on the line.

3. **Catastrophes** such as hurricanes and oil spills have harmed sea life on the coast.

___

Write the missing word.

4. Several sea turtles went on display ______________ they were saved.

after unless although

WEEK 10 DAY 2 Daily Language Review

Write the sentences correctly.

1. Ms. Latimer's class has prepare a holliday concert

___

2. Please to come, enjoy the show, or suport the children.

___

Rewrite this sentence so it is not a fragment.

3. Concert in the cafeteria next Friday 7:00 in the evening

___

Draw a line between the prefix and root word of the underlined word. Then explain what the word means.

4. See our future musical <u>superstars</u> perform.

___

WEEK 10 DAY 3 Daily Language Review

Write the sentences correctly.

1. A solar system has the son and planets that revolve around them.

2. Their are current eight planets in Earth's soler system.

Choose the word that best completes the sentence. Then explain your choice.

3. Pluto used to be called a planet, but it was too ________ to be a planet.

   short tiny brief

Write a sentence from this research note.

4. smallest planet: Mercury

WEEK 10 DAY 4 Daily Language Review

Write the sentences correctly.

1. A Space Needle was built for the 1962 World's Fair in Seattle Washington

2. You can take a elevator but clime 848 steps to the top of the tower.

Use context clues to figure out the meaning of the bold word. Write the meaning on the line.

3. There is a restaurant near the top that **revolves** around the tower.

Write a sentence from this research note.

4. Space Needle: 605 feet high, see the entire city (Seattle)

Read the homophones and their meanings.

ware	something sold at a market
wear	to have on your body
where	at, in, or to a place

Which homophone best completes each sentence?

1. Starting next year, the students must ____________ school uniforms.
2. Erin loves looking at all the different kinds of ____________ at craft fairs.
3. Mikkel dreamed of living ____________ it is warm all year-round.

Write a paragraph using all three homophones.

4. ____

____

____

____

____

____

WEEK 11 DAY 1 Daily Language Review

Write the sentences correctly.

1. My aunt gertie will like to try things which she has never done before.

____

2. She often says “lets have an adventure!”

____

Rewrite the underlined part to put the words in the best order.

3. Last month, we explored a lava huge cave together.

____

Combine the sentences to make one sentence.

4. We could walk in parts of the cave. We crawled in other parts of the cave.

____

WEEK 11 DAY 2 Daily Language Review

Write the sentences correctly.

1. Oh no john exclaimed as he arrives at school without his backpack.

____

2. he runned all the way home, and back to school as fast as he could.

____

Choose the word that best completes the sentence.

3. “Rats!” he ______________ as he searched through his backpack.

asked explained demanded groaned

Write the missing word.

4. John searched and searched, but he ______________ find his history book!

shouldn’t couldn’t won’t

WEEK 11 DAY 3 Daily Language Review

Write the sentences correctly.

1. Eggplant can grow almost anywhere but it like's a lot of Sun.

____

2. Eggplant seed's should be planted, in a place when the soil drains well.

____

Combine the sentences to make one sentence.

3. Some farmers grow eggplant on their farms. The crops grow during the summer months.

____

Rewrite the underlined part to put the words in the best order.

4. <u>Purple nutritious eggplant</u> is a popular food in summer and fall.

____

WEEK 11 DAY 4 Daily Language Review

Write the sentences correctly.

1. Gina and lindsay finish their chores, and wanted to go out.

____

2. They dont want to go somewhere which was far away.

____

Write the missing word.

3. "______________ you like to see the new Star Trek movie?" asked Gina.

   Can   Must   Would

Write the missing interjection.

4. "______________ I was hoping to see that movie," said Lindsay.

   Great!   Nope,   Huh?

Read these words and their meanings.

energetic	having lots of energy
thaw	to melt
depart	to leave

Circle a word in each sentence that means the *opposite* of the underlined word.

1. After the party, the parents were tired, but the children were still energetic.
2. You may freeze the cheesecake, but let it thaw before you serve it.
3. It seemed like just yesterday that my cousin arrived, and already he must depart.

Write a paragraph using at least two of the pairs of *opposite* words.

4. ______________________________

WEEK 12 DAY 1 Daily Language Review

Write the sentences correctly.

1. Have you visit the newer animal on the zoo?

____

2. Crocodiles from Africa eats almost anything that get near their way.

____

Write the missing word.

3. The crocodile mother protects her eggs and helps ____________ hatch.

her it them us

Complete this analogy.

4. shark : fish :: crocodile : ____________

WEEK 12 DAY 2 Daily Language Review

Write the sentences correctly.

1. On July 16 1969, a rocket was launched inside Florida.

____

2. The rocket it reached the moon for days later on Wednesday July 20.

____

Add punctuation to the sentence.

3. Astronauts Neil Armstrong Michael Collins and Buzz Aldrin flew to the moon.

Draw a line between the root word and the suffix of the underlined word. Then explain what the word means.

4. The first moon landing was a <u>memorable</u> day in history.

____

Write the sentences correctly.

1. Some animals stays safe by blending in around its surroundings.

____

2. Skunks don't blend in it is black with white stripes.

____

Write the missing word.

3. Skunks can give off a very powerful ________________ to warn predators.

cent   scent   sent

Write a sentence from this research note.

4. other skunk warnings: stamping feet, hissing

____

Write the sentences correctly.

1. My ant and uncle of Japan has set up an art exhibit of pottery in Dallas.

____

2. In won room of the museum, there is painted bowls teapots and jars.

____

Write the missing word or words.

3. The pottery is painted with the ________________ designs I've ever seen.

most beautiful   beautifulest   most beautifulest

Draw a line between the prefix and the root word of the underlined word. Then explain what the word means.

4. I got to <u>preview</u> the art exhibit the day before it opened.

____

Read these expressions and their meanings.

try	to attempt
try on	to see how a piece of clothing looks on you
try out	to perform so that you may be chosen for a team, a play, or a music group

Which expression best completes each sentence?

1. My cousin wants to ____________________ for the all-star band.
2. The dog ____________________ to dig under the fence, but she couldn't.
3. May I ____________________ that pair of shoes in size 6?

Write a paragraph using all three expressions in the box.

4. ____

____

____

____

____

____

WEEK 13 DAY 1 Daily Language Review

Write the sentences correctly.

1. On October 12 2014, Pauls baseball team faced the Panther's.

____

2. The batter swang at the ball hard but the crowd roared.

____

Use context clues to figure out the meaning of the bold word. Write the meaning on the line.

3. Paul was **distracted** by the crowd and didn't catch the ball.

____

Write the word or words that best complete the sentence. Then explain your choice.

4. Looking at his angry coach, he ______________ another chance to play.

asked for   begged for   requested

____

WEEK 13 DAY 2 Daily Language Review

Write the sentences correctly.

1. Those boys rides the bus two school every day

____

2. Yesterday, they miss the bus because he arrived to early.

____

Write the missing word or words.

3. The boys had to walk a mile to the ______________ city bus stop.

near   nearer   nearest

4. I bet they ______________ up earlier tomorrow!

woke   are waking   will wake

WEEK 13 DAY 3 Daily Language Review

Write the sentences correctly.

1. Brendon found a shortcut threw a field to his best friends' house

___

2. He sees red large patches on his skin unless he started using the shortcut.

___

Use context clues to figure out the meaning of the bold word. Write the meaning on the line.

3. Brendon's mother took him to the **dermatologist** when he developed an itchy rash.

___

Write the missing word or words.

4. The rash ________ out to be poison oak.

turns turned was turning

WEEK 13 DAY 4 Daily Language Review

Write the sentences correctly.

1. Long ago, people wash they're laundry by hand

___

2. They heated water in a tub but rubbed soap on the cloths

___

Rewrite the underlined part to put the words in the best order.

3. Then they rubbed the clothing against a <u>metal bumpy board</u> called a washboard.

___

Write the missing word.

4. Finally, they rinsed the clothing and ________ the clothes out to dry.

hang hanged hung

Read the dictionary entry.

fair
a. honest; right
b. of average quality
c. hair or skin that is light in color
d. clear weather
e. a gathering featuring crafts, rides, competitions, and entertainment; a festival

Which meaning of *fair* is used in the sentence? Write the letter on the line.

1. Unlike the rest of his family, Marco has fair hair. ________
2. Jeff didn't think it was fair to have two tests on the same day. ________
3. Ms. Szabo said that Molly did a fair job on her science report. ________

Write a paragraph using at least three different meanings of the word *fair*.

4. ____

____

____

____

____

____

WEEK 14 DAY 1 Daily Language Review

Write the sentences correctly.

1. My parrott was peck at her food when she sudden looked up.

___

2. She squawked "Danger! help! and hopped up and down.

___

Rewrite this sentence so it is not a fragment.

3. When I looked out the window at a big cat.

___

Write a descriptive word in each blank.

4. The ______ cat jumped ______ over the ______ fence.

WEEK 14 DAY 2 Daily Language Review

Write the sentences correctly.

1. Amelia earhart was born in Atchison Kansas, from 1897.

___

2. She bot for herself a plane for her twenty-fifth birfday.

___

Write a sentence from this research note.

3. Amelia's accomplishments: pilot, teacher, wrote book

___

Draw a line between the prefix and the root word of the underlined word. Then explain what the word means.

4. She was the first woman to make a <u>transatlantic</u> flight alone.

___

WEEK 14 DAY 3 Daily Language Review

Write the sentences correctly.

1. Ron entered a giant-pumpkin contest on Topsfield massachusetts.

 ____

2. Ron's giant pumpkin being a first one to weigh more than one tun.

 ____

Add punctuation to the sentence.

3. Ron said The key to giant pumpkins is Epsom salts and warm water.

Complete this analogy.

4. height : inches :: weight : ______________

WEEK 14 DAY 4 Daily Language Review

Write the sentences correctly.

1. Mr. dunn was talk about fractions when the furnace sudden stopped.

 ____

2. The temperature dropped behind freezing school was canseled.

 ____

Draw a line between the prefix and the root word of the underlined word. Then explain what the word means.

3. The custodian had accidentally <u>disconnected</u> the heat pump.

 ____

Complete this analogy.

4. thermometer : temperature :: clock : ______________

Read these signal words.

yet	after	since
however	later	finally
in contrast	meanwhile	as a result

Which signal word or words best complete each sentence?

1. ____________________ my mom comes home at night, she doesn't like to go out again.

2. ____________________, our family doesn't eat out very often.

3. ____________________, our neighbors have been to every restaurant in the city.

Write a paragraph using at least three signal words from the box.

4. ____

____

____

____

____

____

WEEK 15 DAY 1 Daily Language Review

Write the sentences correctly.

1. We were look forward to spending the day, at the amusement park.

____

2. It has the world's taller Roller Coaster, that is called Kingda Ka.

____

Write the missing word.

3. We ____________ go until Dad remembered where the car keys were.

   shouldn't couldn't can't

Write the word that best completes the sentence. Then explain your choice.

4. He finally found the keys on Mom's ____________ desk, and we left.

   dusty messy dirty polluted

____

WEEK 15 DAY 2 Daily Language Review

Write the sentences correctly.

1. My father listening to the weather report while making lunch for he and I.

____

2. A Tornado was came, and it could be big than the last one.

____

Combine the sentences to make one sentence.

3. The tornado damaged many homes. It missed the elementary school.

____

Draw a line between the root word and the suffix of the underlined word. Then explain what the word means.

4. We were <u>thankful</u> that no one was hurt.

____

Write the sentences correctly.

1. People that think that all dinosaures were huge are wrong.

____

2. There was one dinosaur, who was only as big such as a turkey.

____

Combine the sentences to make one sentence.

3. The compsognathus was a swift hunter. It was a deadly hunter.

____

Write the plural of each underlined noun.

4. It caught and held its <u>prey</u> with its three-fingered <u>hand</u> and sharp <u>tooth</u>.

_______________ _______________ _______________

Write the sentences correctly.

1. My brother, he always experimenting in the kitchen.

____

2. He invented a milkshake flavor who he called, "lemon lima bean."

____

Write the word that best completes the sentence. Then explain your choice.

3. While I took just a little swallow, he _______________ a whole glass.

sipped tasted guzzled tried

____

Write the missing word.

4. "This is my _______________ creation yet!" he exclaimed.

tasty tastiest tastier

Read these related words and their meanings.

encourage *verb*
to urge someone to do something; to try to make something happen

encouragement *noun*
words or actions that give hope or confidence

encouraging *adjective*
causing feelings of hope or confidence

Which word best completes each sentence?

1. Tony felt like quitting, but the team's ____________ made him try again.
2. The ____________ news made the patient smile.
3. I ____________ you to be as creative as you can.

Write a paragraph using all three related words.

4. ____

____

____

____

____

____

WEEK 16 DAY 1 Daily Language Review

Write the sentences correctly.

1. Me and him have spend the weekend at camerons cabin.

____

2. First we had a cookout but later we told ghost stories.

____

Use context clues to figure out the meaning of the bold word. Write the meaning on the line.

3. The next day we hiked and nearly fell off a 100-foot **precipice**!

____

Draw a line between the root word and the suffix of the underlined word. Then explain what the word means.

4. Such a long plunge would have been <u>disastrous</u>.

____

WEEK 16 DAY 2 Daily Language Review

Write the sentences correctly.

1. Sylvia had wait all year for our peach tree to bare fruit.

____

2. Her and their sister was ready to gather they're harvest.

____

Rewrite the underlined part to put the words in the best order.

3. Finally, Sylvia picked the first <u>ripe delicious peach</u> from the tree.

____

Choose the correct word to complete this analogy.

4. fruit : juicy :: nut : ____________________

   a. shell   b. crunchy   c. eat

WEEK 16 DAY 3 Daily Language Review

Write the sentences correctly.

1. Have you ever try to make applesauce youself?

____

2. You puts apple slices in a pot add water and cook it.

____

Add punctuation to the sentence.

3. Three good types of apples for applesauce are Gala Fuji and Golden Delicious.

Complete this analogy.

4. cinnamon : spice :: fork : ____________________

WEEK 16 DAY 4 Daily Language Review

Write the sentences correctly.

1. The statue of liberty were a gift from france.

____

2. The statues symbolism represents freedom friendship or democracy.

____

Rewrite the underlined part to put the words in the best order.

3. The statue was placed on a <u>stone large base</u>.

____

Use context clues to figure out the meaning of the bold word. Write the meaning on the line.

4. The statue celebrated the 1876 **centennial** of the Declaration of Independence.

____

Read the homophones and their meanings.

right	correct or best; the direction opposite of *left*
rite	an act that is part of a ceremony; an important event in a person's life
write	to state in words on paper or in a text or e-mail

Which homophone best completes each sentence?

1. Sara and Bill always ____________________ thank-you notes when they receive a gift.
2. It can take awhile to choose the ____________________ career.
3. Lighting candles is a common wedding ____________________.

Write a paragraph using all three homophones.

4. ____

____

____

____

____

____

WEEK 17 DAY 1 Daily Language Review

Write the sentences correctly.

1. Perry climed across the tall ladder to the diving board

____

2. Wow Perry, that diving board is high shouts Carmen.

____

Write the missing interjection.

3. "______________ I'm so used to it that I don't think about it anymore."

Uh-oh, Rats! Look! Gee,

Explain how interjections help in dialogue.

4. Interjections ______________________________

____

WEEK 17 DAY 2 Daily Language Review

Write the sentences correctly.

1. Ouch I can't get the TV to work complained Meg

____

2. Meg firm pressed a power button in the remote control

____

Write a descriptive word in each blank.

3. John moved the ______________ TV to the side and saw the ______________ cord hanging down.

Write the missing word.

4. "It ______________ have come unplugged when I vacuumed," said John.

can must would should

WEEK 17 DAY 3 Daily Language Review

Write the sentences correctly.

1. Drinking enaugh water every day is importantly to your health.

___

2. Water helped take toxins out your body and helps make blood flow easily

___

Rewrite this sentence so it is not a run-on sentence.

3. Water reduces the chance of a heart attack it prevents some cancers.

___

Write a sentence from this research note.

4. water benefits: muscle health, prevents cramps

___

WEEK 17 DAY 4 Daily Language Review

Write the sentences correctly.

1. Next month, I am moved to Bozeman Montana and want to learn about it

___

2. Please to describe all an elemetary schools at the area.

___

Rewrite this sentence so it is not a fragment.

3. For instance, any sports, arts, or science programs?

___

Write the missing word.

4. I ________________ like to get involved quickly.

could can must would

Read these words and their meanings.

secure	protected from danger or harm
pastime	an activity you like to do in your free time
wonder	to be curious about something

Circle a word in each sentence that has a meaning *similar* to the underlined word.

1. The bank's website has been made more secure, so customers should feel safe using it.
2. Alejandro has many hobbies, but his favorite pastime is horseback riding.
3. The kindergartners know that there are stars in the night sky, but they wonder where the stars go during the day.

Write a paragraph using at least two of the pairs of *similar* words.

4. ______________________________

____

____

____

____

____

WEEK 18 DAY 1 Daily Language Review

Write the sentences correctly.

1. "Hooray! That was the worse sandwich I ever eaten," said Kyle.

____

2. Kyle drank two glass's of milk, to get rid of the bad taste.

____

Draw a line between the prefix and the root word of the underlined word. Then explain what the word means.

3. The sandwich was <u>overstuffed</u> and soggy.

____

Rewrite this sentence so it is not a fragment.

4. The meat not being fresh, either.

____

WEEK 18 DAY 2 Daily Language Review

Write the sentences correctly.

1. Whales are more like human's, than you might have thinked.

____

2. Whales breathe air since they live in the Ocean.

____

Combine the sentences to make one sentence.

3. Some whales sing. These are blue whales and humpback whales.

____

Rewrite this sentence so it is not a run-on sentence.

4. Whales are not fish they are mammals, just like people are.

____

WEEK 18 DAY 3 Daily Language Review

Write the sentences correctly.

1. On December 14 1911, five explorer's first reached, the South Pole.

____

2. Hawaii been a State since August 21 1959.

____

Write the missing word.

3. Slavery ended ______________ the Thirteenth Amendment passed in 1865.

until   although   when   while

Combine the sentences to make one sentence.

4. World War II lasted for six years. World War II ended in 1945.

____

WEEK 18 DAY 4 Daily Language Review

Write the sentences correctly.

1. On Sunday December 28, it rained heavily, in Foggy Gap.

____

2. It was the most biggest Storm which the area had ever saw.

____

Write an appropriate interjection.

3. "______________ We never see this much rain," exclaimed Sergio.

Write the word that best completes the sentence. Then explain your choice.

4. The roads and the ground are absolutely ______________ from the storm.

moist   soaked   damp   wet

____

Read these expressions and their meanings.

hang	to attach something on a wall or a high place
hang on	to wait a short time
hang up	to end a phone call

Which expression best completes each sentence?

1. If you can ____________________ another minute, I'll find that book for you.
2. I will go to the store as soon as we ____________________.
3. Please ____________________ your coat on the hook by the door.

Write a paragraph using all three expressions from the box.

4. ____

____

____

____

____

____

WEEK 19 DAY 1 Daily Language Review

Write the sentences correctly.

1. Eric didnt prepare good for his report on the civil war.

___

2. He writed his notes real quick the knight before the report was due.

___

Add punctuation to the sentence.

3. In addition he stayed up late playing video games

What does the underlined phrase mean?

4. Listening to his report was <u>as interesting as watching paint dry</u>.

___

WEEK 19 DAY 2 Daily Language Review

Write the sentences correctly.

1. Aunt evelyn has works as a Police Officer for ten years.

___

2. She has live in Ames, Iowa; hilo, Hawaii, and Dayton ohio.

___

Write the missing word.

3. She is the person ________ inspires me the most.

whom who which

Add punctuation to the sentence.

4. When I am older I want to help keep the public safe.

WEEK 19 DAY 3 Daily Language Review

Write the sentences correctly.

1. There are several commonly fears whom many people have.

____

2. Do you know anyone whom is fearfully of spiders.

____

What does the underlined phrase mean?

3. Terry is <u>a real chicken</u> when it comes to heights.

____

Write the missing word.

4. Samantha is scared ____________________ she has to talk to a large group.

when where who

WEEK 19 DAY 4 Daily Language Review

Write the sentences correctly.

1. When we think of antarctica we think of very cold whether.

____

2. Ice sheets move slow from inland areas, to the see.

____

Draw a line between the root word and the suffix of the underlined word. Then explain what the word means.

3. The mountains, plains, and coastlines are all <u>icy</u>.

____

Add punctuation to the sentence.

4. Antarctica is even colder than Siberia Russia

Read the dictionary entry.

pound a. a weight equal to 16 ounces
b. a place that keeps stray animals
c. a unit of money used in the United Kingdom
d. the symbol #; hashtag
e. to hit hard over and over

Which meaning of *pound* is used in the sentence? Write the letter on the line.

1. Dad always pounds the steaks to make them tender. ______
2. I can buy that book online for only 4 pounds. ______
3. Enter your account number, followed by the pound sign. ______

Write a paragraph using at least three different meanings of the word *pound*.

4. ______________________________

WEEK 20 DAY 1 Daily Language Review

Write the sentences correctly.

1. "Hey Mom can we go camping when school is out asked Juan"

____

2. We discussed going camping in August didn't we? Mom replied

____

Write the missing word.

3. "I ______________ like to go in June instead," Juan stated.

must would can

The Latin root *loc* means "place." What does the bold word in the sentence probably mean?

4. "I will look for a **location** we can camp at in June," responded Mom.

____

WEEK 20 DAY 2 Daily Language Review

Write the sentences correctly.

1. Astronomers says there going to be a shower of falling stars tonite.

____

2. Actually falling stars is bits of space dirt falling to Earth

____

Write the missing word.

3. Some pieces of space dirt are no ______________ than a grain of sand.

large larger largest

Combine the sentences to make one sentence.

4. The space dirt burns up when it enters the sky. We see a light in the sky.

____

WEEK 20 DAY 3 Daily Language Review

Write the sentences correctly.

1. One of the popularest pets are a fish

____

2. Some types of fish lives in fresh water and some prefer salty water

____

Write the missing word.

3. To keep fish as pets, you ______________ feed them and clean their tank.

might must could

The Latin root *aqua* means "water." What does the bold word in the sentence probably mean?

4. Don't put too many fish in your **aquarium**, or they will be crowded.

____

WEEK 20 DAY 4 Daily Language Review

Write the sentences correctly.

1. In Brazil the tropical rich rainforests are disappear.

____

2. Rainforests are a important part of the enviroment on Erth.

____

Combine the sentences to make one sentence.

3. Trees give off oxygen. We need oxygen to breathe.

____

Write the missing word or words.

4. The trees in a rainforest ______________ homes for many animals.

provide provides are provided

Read these signal words.

for instance	such as	likewise
to begin with	specifically	that is
on one hand	instead	additionally

Which signal word or words best complete each sentence?

1. How do you learn a new difficult skill ____________ playing the piano?
2. ____________, you should find a good teacher and take lessons.
3. ____________, practicing every day will help you achieve your goal.

Write a paragraph using at least three signal words from the box.

4. ____

____

____

____

____

____

WEEK 21 DAY 1 Daily Language Review

Write the sentences correctly.

1. I were doing our homework after school since I heard a noise.

2. I couldnt figure out what the noise was but I went back to my book.

Choose the word that best completes the sentence.

3. I looked up when I heard a light ____________ on the glass.

   knocking pounding tapping banging

Combine the sentences to make one sentence.

4. There was a little bird outside the window. The bird wanted to come in.

WEEK 21 DAY 2 Daily Language Review

Write the sentences correctly.

1. When Chelsea was on a trip to Dorset Vermont they saw snow for the first time.

2. When she looked out the planes window everything were white.

Choose the word that best completes the sentence. Then explain your choice.

3. "I can't wait to build a snowman!" Chelsea ____________ to her parents.

   complained suggested announced

Add punctuation to the sentence.

4. "Its mighty cold! Bundle up Chelsea," her parents warned.

WEEK 21 DAY 3 Daily Language Review

Write the sentences correctly.

1. Englands laws is made by a group called parliament.

2. Parliament is located to the Palace of westminster in London England.

Use context clues to figure out the meaning of the bold word. Write the meaning on the line.

3. Some members of Parliament are elected, while others are **appointed** by royalty.

The Latin root *equ* means "same." What does the bold word in the sentence probably mean?

4. England's Parliament is **equivalent** to the United States' Congress.

WEEK 21 DAY 4 Daily Language Review

Write the sentences correctly.

1. Six months ago cecilia began playing the flute in their schools orchestra.

2. Tonight she are performing into a concert at highland elementary school.

What does the underlined phrase mean?

3. She dresses as quick as a wink and hurries off to the concert.

Add punctuation to the sentence.

4. "You arent nervous are you?" Cecilias mother asks.

Read these related words and their meanings.

music *noun*
sounds that go together well that are made by singing or instruments

musician *noun*
a person who plays music

musical *adjective*
having a talent for music; related to music

Which word best completes each sentence?

1. Richard discovered that he liked violin ______________ when he was four years old.
2. Laurie performs in ______________ theater every chance she has.
3. Steve would like to be a professional ______________ someday.

Write a paragraph using all three related words.

4. ______________________________

WEEK 22 DAY 1 Daily Language Review

Write the sentences correctly.

1. Mr. Chang was save his money to buy a car which was gooder then his old one.

2. Last week, he looks at all the adds and chose a green sports stylish car.

What does the underlined phrase mean?

3. The new car turned out to be a lemon.

What does the underlined proverb mean?

4. The next time he chooses a car, he will look before he leaps.

WEEK 22 DAY 2 Daily Language Review

Write the sentences correctly.

1. "I'm have a party on Saturday Febuary 1 announced Mei-Lin.

2. "I am invited aren't I? asked Debbie."

Rewrite this sentence so it is not a run-on sentence.

3. "Of course that's why I'm telling you about it!" said Mei-Lin.

What does the underlined phrase mean?

4. "You can count me in!" replied Debbie.

WEEK 22 DAY 3 Daily Language Review

Write the sentences correctly.

1. The first modern Olympic Games, they taked place on April 6 1896.

___

2. Men competed in sports such as track restling and gimnastics.

___

The Greek root *athl* means "contest." What does the bold word in the sentence probably mean?

3. **Athletes** from 14 countries participated in the first modern Olympic Games.

___

Write the missing word.

4. ___ could not take part in the Olympic Games until 1900.

Wimen Weman Women

WEEK 22 DAY 4 Daily Language Review

Write the sentences correctly.

1. Gina's father makes the tastier Italian food which she has ever eaten.

___

2. Papa said Let's make the filling pasta and sauce for ravioli together.

___

Write the missing word.

3. Gina read the ___ and said that it looked hard.

recipe recipie recipy

What does the underlined adage mean?

4. Papa reminded her that <u>practice makes perfect</u>.

___

Read the homophones and their meanings.

oar	a long stick used for rowing and steering a boat; a paddle
or	a word used to show another choice or option
ore	rock containing valuable metal

Which homophone best completes each sentence?

1. We can go white-water rafting ______________ kayaking.
2. Peter Doroshin found ______________ with gold nuggets 47 years before the Yukon Gold Rush began.
3. Elaine slowly pulled an ______________ through the water and started moving across the lake.

Write a paragraph using all three homophones.

4. ______________________________

WEEK 23 DAY 1 Daily Language Review

Write the sentences correctly.

1. Mercury is just a little large than Earths moon.

2. One of Mercurys Days are about as long as 58 days in Earth.

What does the underlined phrase mean?

3. Mercury rotates on its axis slowly but orbits the sun <u>like a race car</u>.

The Latin root *sol* means "sun." What does the bold word in the sentence probably mean?

4. Mercury is the smallest planet in our **solar** system.

WEEK 23 DAY 2 Daily Language Review

Write the sentences correctly.

1. If you've ever had an headache you knows it can be caused by many things.

2. For instance headache's can be caused by, a cold or badly posture.

Use context clues to figure out the meaning of the bold word. Write the meaning on the line.

3. Your headache may go away if you **recline** on the bed and close your eyes.

Rewrite the sentence to put the words in the best order.

4. You can also try doing neck slow stretches to relieve the pain.

WEEK 23 DAY 3 Daily Language Review

Write the sentences correctly.

1. Several deers was nibbling grass on the park next my house.

____

2. All of a sudden an deer walked between the street, stopped, and looked around.

____

Rewrite the sentence so that it is not a fragment.

3. A new black pick-up truck that came speeding down the road.

____

What does the underlined phrase mean?

4. Fortunately, the truck was able to stop on a dime.

____

WEEK 23 DAY 4 Daily Language Review

Write the sentences correctly.

1. Long ago there was no weekends, and Holidays were the only breaks from work.

____

2. Much holidays was created to celebrate the changing of the Seasons.

____

Use context clues to figure out the meaning of the bold word. Write the meaning on the line.

3. Holidays involve certain foods and **rituals** such as giving gifts or lighting candles.

____

Complete this analogy.

4. flag : Independence Day :: turkey : _______________

Read these words and their meanings.

opponent	a person or team that you work or compete against
worthless	having no value; not good for anything
steep	at an angle with a high slope

Circle a word in each sentence that means the *opposite* of the underlined word.

1. After Jack's team won the game, his teammates hugged each other while their opponents looked sad.
2. The first app Dad bought was worthless, but the second one was very useful.
3. It's much more fun to skateboard down steep roads than on flat ones.

Write a paragraph using at least two of the pairs of *opposite* words.

4. ______________________________

____

____

____

____

____

WEEK 24 DAY 1 Daily Language Review

Write the sentences correctly.

1. In 1767, John Spilsbury was working as a Mapmaker in London England

   ____

2. John wanted to teach geography in a fun way as they made the first jigsaw puzzle.

   ____

Write the missing word or words.

3. The first puzzle was a world map, ______________ it was made of wood.

   if and so when

4. Cardboard ______________ used to make puzzles since the late 1800s.

   is has been was being

WEEK 24 DAY 2 Daily Language Review

Write the sentences correctly.

1. To get a well job you should have the college education.

   ____

2. College students get to choose, which classes you take

   ____

Write the missing word or words.

3. ______________ college can be difficult, it is worth the effort.

   Even though Unless Whenever

The Latin root *schola* means "school." What does the bold word in the sentence probably mean?

4. Most colleges have programs to help new **scholars** adjust to college life.

   ____

WEEK 24 DAY 3 Daily Language Review

Write the sentences correctly.

1. At last week's diving competition Dimitry climbs up the highly ladder.

____

2. Then he will walk to the end of the diving board, and bounced on it alot.

____

Write the missing word.

3. He pictured the dive in his head ____________ he jumped off the board.

as yet unless

What does the underlined phrase mean?

4. When the diver entered the water, his body was <u>as straight as an arrow</u>.

____

WEEK 24 DAY 4 Daily Language Review

Write the sentences correctly.

1. We have plan our year vacation to Scotland

____

2. The last time we go we visit my aunt, but she has move away since then.

____

Write a descriptive word in each blank.

3. We hope we will see many ____________ castles and ____________ museums.

Add punctuation to the sentence.

4. Our trip will last from May 29 2016 to June 29 2016

Read these expressions and their meanings.

feel blue	to be sad
blue in the face	exhausted
once in a blue moon	rarely; with lots of time in between

Which expression best completes each sentence?

1. She argued until she was ______________________ but didn't change anyone's mind.
2. After moving to Vermont, he ______________________ when he thought of his old home.
3. I get to see my grandparents only ______________________.

Write a paragraph using all three expressions from the box.

4. ____

____

____

____

____

____

WEEK 25 DAY 1 Daily Language Review

Write the sentences correctly.

1. Hey our washing mashine isn't working properly", said Malia.

____

2. Even though they tried niether my mom or my dad could fix it themselves.

____

Rewrite this sentence so it is not a run-on sentence.

3. They went to a store they found a new one they liked but it was too expensive.

____

Use context clues to figure out the meaning of the bold word. Write the meaning on the line.

4. That **tenacious** salesman just wouldn't take no for an answer.

____

WEEK 25 DAY 2 Daily Language Review

Write the sentences correctly.

1. A munth ago an alarm went off at the Smith Brother's Market.

____

2. When they heard the loud nois both my dog or my cat reacted to it.

____

Write the missing words.

3. Someone _______________ their computers and the store's cash register.

wearing black   had stolen   very quickly

Use context clues to figure out the meaning of the bold word. Write the meaning on the line.

4. Police arrested the **perpetrator** of the crime later that week.

____

Write the sentences correctly.

1. Ben Jerry and Albert read a scarey book called Infestation by Timothy Bradley.

2. The scarier book which Marcus ever read was The Monsters of Morley Manor.

Add punctuation to the sentence.

3. Jan likes books by Lois Lowry Grace Lin and Charlotte Emily and Anne Brontë.

The Latin root *littera* means "letter." What does the bold word in the sentence probably mean?

4. Akiko enjoys reading Greek **literature** about the ancient world.

Write the sentences correctly,

1. "Grandpa come out and kick soccor balls around with us said Hyson."

2. "You know that soccer hurts my knees dont you? Grandpa responded.

Rewrite this sentence so it is not a run-on sentence.

3. "Then let's all go for a walk we just want to spend time with you," Hyson offered.

Use context clues to figure out the meaning of the bold word. Write the meaning on the line.

4. "That's very **considerate** of you to change your plans just for me!" Grandpa said.

Read the dictionary entry.

match
a. a short stick used to light a fire
b. a contest in a sport or game
c. a competitor who is just as good as his or her opponent
d. to look just like something else
e. to go together well

Which meaning of *match* is used in the sentence? Write the letter on the line.

1. This chair matches the style of Erino's bedroom. ______
2. After Greg's first chess move, Brad knew he had met his match. ______
3. The team won four matches at the state championship. ______

Write a paragraph using at least three different meanings of the word *match*.

4. ______________________________

WEEK 26 DAY 1 Daily Language Review

Write the sentences correctly.

1. Upon the United States there's many people involved in making laws.

____

2. To make a new law both the House of Representatives but also the Senate has to agree.

____

Write the missing words.

3. Each group ______________________ changes in the wording.

discuss and suggest   discusses and suggest   discusses and suggests

The Latin root *ann* means "year." What does the bold word in the sentence probably mean?

4. There are usually over 200 laws passed **annually**.

____

WEEK 26 DAY 2 Daily Language Review

Write the sentences correctly.

1. Mario haven't try any winter sports after moving to Michigan.

____

2. At Sunday March 2 he went to an ice-skating party.

____

Write the missing word.

3. Mario ______________ have had a great time at the party.

can   will   must

What does the underlined phrase mean?

4. Now Mario flies across the ice <u>like a supersonic jet</u>.

____

WEEK 26 DAY 3 Daily Language Review

Write the sentences correctly.

1. My English class are read the famous poem Casey at the Bat.

____

2. A newspaper called The San Francisco Examiner published the poem June 3 1888.

____

Write the missing word.

3. A comedian read the poem in a show _______________ he saw it in the paper.

after   unless   yet

What does the underlined phrase mean?

4. The audience loved it, and the poem took off <u>like wildfire</u>.

____

WEEK 26 DAY 4 Daily Language Review

Write the sentences correctly.

1. When Susie was grow up she lived in a ranch beneath two rivers in Montana.

____

2. She had always want to take a trip toward neither New York City or Los Angeles.

____

Add punctuation to the sentence.

3. She went to visit her cousins in New York City on December 21 2015.

Choose the word that best completes the sentence. Then explain your choice.

4. Susie _______________ in awe at all the giant buildings surrounding her.

peeked   stared   glared

____

Read these signal words.

until	furthermore	simultaneously
whenever	surely	during
so far	in addition	afterward

Which signal word or words best complete each sentence?

1. ____________________ my aunt visits, she likes to try new things.
2. ____________________ to my aunt trying them, she expects me to as well.
3. ____________________, all the activities have been quite fun.

Write a paragraph using at least three signal words from the box.

4. ____

____

____

____

____

____

WEEK 27 DAY 1 Daily Language Review

Write the sentences correctly.

1. Last weekend Geeta and I read a article called No Uniforms in School.

____

2. I telled Geeta The author didn't make a very well argument did she?

____

Write the missing word or words.

3. Geeta ______________ enjoyed the article, but she also agreed with it.

either neither not not only

What does the underlined proverb mean?

4. Instead of arguing about it, we'll just live and let live.

____

WEEK 27 DAY 2 Daily Language Review

Write the sentences correctly.

1. There is a speshal assembly at Oak hills elementary school last monday.

____

2. The elkhorn Orkestra played music from the musical The wizard of oz.

____

The Latin root *aud* means "hear." What does the bold word in the sentence probably mean?

3. Music filled the **auditorium** as the musicians began playing.

____

Combine the sentences to make one sentence.

4. The concert ended. The audience clapped loudly.

____

Write the sentences correctly.

1. "At soccer we practiced dribbling passing and receiving drills", said Miguel.

2. Look! That sounds like a exausting afternoon! Dad responded.

Write the missing word.

3. Miguel complained that his ________________ have never been so sore before.

   mussels muscels muscles mustles

What does the underlined adage mean?

4. Dad said, "I know you're tired, but <u>no pain, no gain</u>."

Write the sentences correctly.

1. Astronot neil armstrong begins flying when he was 16 years old.

2. Armstrong became a Navy pilot serves in the korean war and went to college.

Add punctuation to the sentence.

3. When Armstrong landed on the moon he said That's one small step for man, one giant leap for mankind.

The Latin root *lun* means "moon." What does the bold word in the sentence probably mean?

4. Armstrong became the first human to step on the **lunar** surface.

Read these related words and their meanings.

autograph *noun*
a person's written signature

paragraph *noun*
a short piece of writing on one subject

photograph *noun*
a picture taken by a camera

Which word best completes each sentence?

1. Our essays have to be four ____________________ long.
2. That ____________________ shows my grandfather when he was a young boy.
3. The band members signed ____________________ after the concert.

Write a paragraph using all three related words.

4. ____

____

____

____

____

____

WEEK 28 DAY 1 Daily Language Review

Write the sentences correctly.

1. Whether you cooks them and eat them raw vegetables and fruit is good for you.

____

2. Foods of different colors has different nutrients but there all healthy.

____

Write the missing word.

3. If you don't like veggies, you ____________ mix them with foods you like.

would should will

Rewrite the sentence to put the words in the best order.

4. You should try some Thai delicious food the next time you eat out.

____

WEEK 28 DAY 2 Daily Language Review

Write the sentences correctly.

1. Our science class are studying the magnetic large field around Earth.

____

2. Yesterday, we watched a short Video who was called Our Planet Is a Magnet.

____

Write the missing word.

3. It showed an experiment that was neither interesting ____________ clear.

or but nor

Use context clues to figure out the meaning of the bold word. Write the meaning on the line.

4. Even the teacher was **perplexed** by the difficult science experiment.

____

WEEK 28 DAY 3 Daily Language Review

Write the sentences correctly.

1. Josie and Uncle Lee is making a cake from a Book called Easy Cakes at Home.

____

2. "Uncle Lee all this cake batter, mustn't fit in the pan will it?" asked Josie.

____

The Greek root *metron* means "measure." What does the bold word in the sentence probably mean?

3. "Make sure you use a round cake pan with the right **diameter**," said Uncle Lee.

____

Complete this analogy.

4. pint : volume :: inch : ____________

WEEK 28 DAY 4 Daily Language Review

Write the sentences correctly.

1. "There's only two days left to finish our report or they will be late," said Afshin.

____

2. "We could use another weak to right the report couldn't I?" replied Justin.

____

Write the missing word.

3. "____________ we just ask Mr. Wu for one more day?" continued Justin.

Can't Mustn't Wouldn't

What does the underlined phrase mean?

4. "He made the due date for the report crystal clear," Afshin reminded him.

____

Read the homophones and their meanings.

chord	a set of musical notes played at the same time
cord	a thick string; electric wire wrapped in plastic
cored	past tense of *to core*: to remove the core from a piece of fruit

Which homophone best completes each sentence?

1. The last ____________________ of the song sounded surprising.
2. Alissa ____________________ the apples before slicing them.
3. Make sure the power ____________________ is plugged in correctly.

Write a paragraph using all three homophones.

4. ____

____

____

____

____

____

WEEK 29 DAY 1 Daily Language Review

Write the sentences correctly.

1. The mountain with the higher altitude on Earth, it's Mount Everest

____

2. From its underwater base Mauna Kea is actually more taller than Mount Everest

____

Write the missing word.

3. ______________ Mount Everest and Mauna Kea attract many climbers.

Either Both Neither Not

Draw a line between the prefix and the root word of the underlined word. Then explain what the word means.

4. If you want to climb Mount Everest, be prepared for <u>subzero</u> temperatures.

____

WEEK 29 DAY 2 Daily Language Review

Write the sentences correctly.

1. Yesterday in music class we sing a round called Are You Sleeping

____

2. Today we are practice a round being Row, Row, Row Your Boat.

____

Write the missing word or words.

3. Next week, we ______________ about famous composers.

had learned have learned will learn

4. My favorite composer is ______________ Bach or Brahms.

either neither not only

WEEK 29 DAY 3 Daily Language Review

Write the sentences correctly.

1. Mariselas family move from Dallas Texas to Edmonds Washington back in June.

___

2. When she first started at our new school it seemed difficulter than their old one

___

Rewrite this sentence so it is not a run-on sentence.

3. Then she learned her way around she made new friends she joined a club.

___

What does the underlined proverb mean?

4. Marisela realized that <u>you shouldn't judge a book by its cover.</u>

___

WEEK 29 DAY 4 Daily Language Review

Write the sentences correctly.

1. Ms. Chen driving to work when she sawd three calfs in the middle of the road.

___

2. The animales just standed there staring at Ms. Chens car.

___

What does the underlined phrase mean?

3. "This delay could <u>put a dent in</u> my schedule," she sighed.

___

Rewrite this sentence so it is not a run-on sentence.

4. Eventually, a rancher came by he herded them back to his ranch.

___

Read these words and their meanings.

career	a type of work or business; a profession
bicker	to argue about little things
frigid	extremely cold

Circle a word in each sentence that has a meaning *similar* to the underlined word.

1. Uncle Marvin's high school job painting houses led to his career as an architect.
2. Haley never really fought with her brother, but they did bicker about doing chores.
3. It gets chilly during winter here in Oregon, but I've heard it gets frigid in Wisconsin.

Write a paragraph using at least two of the pairs of *similar* words.

4. ____

____

____

____

____

____

WEEK 30 DAY 1 Daily Language Review

Write the sentences correctly.

1. The Armenta's needed a vacuum cleaner which would neither clog or overheat.

____

2. They read an Article on Consumer Reports about the goodest vacuum cleaners.

____

Add punctuation to the sentence.

3. The article in the May 1 2011 edition was called Putting Vacuum Cleaners to the Test.

Choose the word that best completes the sentence. Then explain your choice.

4. The new vacuum cleaner does a good job of ____________ the carpet.

scouring   polishing   cleaning

____

WEEK 30 DAY 2 Daily Language Review

Write the sentences correctly.

1. "Dad Marco and I are going out to play ball okay?" Kerry said to his Father.

____

2. The Boys went at the backyard to practice, throwing catching and batting.

____

Choose the word that best completes the sentence. Then explain your choice.

3. When the baseball ____________ the window, the glass broke.

tapped   struck   beat

____

Complete this analogy.

4. referee : whistle :: catcher : ____________

WEEK 30 DAY 3 Daily Language Review

Write the sentences correctly.

1. Have You ever be afraid about something for no good reason?

____

2. Many people fear spiders snakes or dogs even if they never been bitten.

____

Combine the sentences to make one sentence.

3. Other people fear doing certain things. They might be afraid to speak in public.

____

The Greek root *phob* means "fear." What does the bold word in the sentence probably mean?

4. Surprisingly, many pilots have a **phobia** of heights.

____

WEEK 30 DAY 4 Daily Language Review

Write the sentences correctly.

1. Computers have change a lot until the 1980s haven't they?

____

2. Long ago, Apps were upon square large disks that you put onto the computer.

____

Combine the sentences to make one sentence.

3. Back then, computers didn't use a mouse. You had to type to open a file.

____

Explain how prepositional phrases can make sentences better.

4. Prepositional phrases ____

____

Read these expressions and their meanings.

know it by heart	to have something memorized
take heart	to relax and not worry
take it to heart	to really understand and believe something

Which expression best completes each sentence?

1. Marta loves the song "Fifty Nifty United States" and ______________________.
2. I listened to the doctor's advice and ______________________.
3. After the frost killed our apple tree, Dad said to ______________________, because it will grow back in spring.

Write a paragraph using all three expressions from the box.

4. ____

____

____

____

____

____

WEEK 31 DAY 1 Daily Language Review

Write the sentences correctly.

1. The weather were perfectly for the beach volleyball tournament.

___

2. "They've been playing a exciting game havent they? the announcer commented."

___

Use context clues to figure out the meaning of the bold word. Write the meaning on the line.

3. The athletes became concerned when they saw the dark, **ominous** sky.

___

Write the missing interjection.

4. "___" said the announcer as the rain suddenly poured down.

What a pity! Well done! Whew!

WEEK 31 DAY 2 Daily Language Review

Write the sentences correctly.

1. Either Toy Story or The Incredibles are Carolinas favorite movie.

___

2. She like to have popcorn candy and neither a soda or a lemonade at the theater.

___

Write the missing word.

3. ___ I go with her or not, she sees a movie every week.

Either Neither Whether

What does the underlined phrase mean?

4. Carolina is as happy as a purring kitten when she watches a movie.

___

WEEK 31 DAY 3 Daily Language Review

Write the sentences correctly.

1. The United States became a country in 1776 but there were no president.

 ____

2. Who led a country before George Washington took office on April 30 1789?

 ____

Write the missing word.

3. The Continental Congress was in charge of the country both during ______________ after the Revolutionary War.

 or and but

Use context clues to figure out the meaning of the bold word. Write the meaning on the line.

4. They wrote the Constitution, which **specifies** that a president runs the country.

 ____

WEEK 31 DAY 4 Daily Language Review

Write the sentences correctly.

1. "Hey Jeffrey is Auckland the capital of New Zealand? asked Fernando."

 ____

2. "No its Wellington, at the south end of the North Island Jeffrey responded.

 ____

Write a descriptive word in each blank.

3. Fernando ______________ admired his ______________ friend.

What does the underlined phrase mean?

4. Jeffrey is <u>a walking atlas</u>.

 ____

Read the dictionary entry.

treat a. a special food or snack
b. something nice that doesn't happen often
c. to act a certain way toward someone or something
d. to pay for someone else's meal or ticket
e. to give medical care

Which meaning of *treat* is used in the sentence? Write the letter on the line.

1. Ms. Ming treats all of her students with respect. ______
2. When we visit my uncle, he will treat us to a Broadway show. ______
3. It was such a treat to go horseback riding. ______

Write a paragraph using at least three different meanings of the word *treat*.

4. ______________________________

____

____

____

____

____

WEEK 32 DAY 1 Daily Language Review

Write the sentences correctly.

1. My brother gave I his sleeping old brown bag for my first camping trip.

____

2. I went with my school's sience club to a camp in san bernardino california.

____

Write the missing word or words.

3. We ______________ to our tent when we heard a strange sound.

have hiked   hike   were hiking

4. There was a bear ______________ in the trees behind us!

rustling   russelling   wrusling

WEEK 32 DAY 2 Daily Language Review

Write the sentences correctly.

1. "You're exited about going to Washington D.C. aren't you?" Eric asked.

____

2. Of course, Eric. I am pack right now," said jimmy.

____

Write the missing word.

3. "We ______________ miss our train if we don't leave soon," Eric warned.

should   might   must

Draw a line between the root word and the suffix of the underlined word. Then explain what the word means.

4. Soon they were headed <u>northward</u> for their big train trip.

____

WEEK 32 DAY 3 Daily Language Review

Write the sentences correctly.

1. I am read the book island of the blue dolphins right now.

____

2. it's about a girl that gets left behind after all the villiagers leave the island.

____

Write the missing word or words.

3. She _______________ take care of herself because she is all alone.

   would   might   has to

4. The story takes place on _______________ in California.

   san Nicolas Island   San Nicolas Island   San Nicolas island

WEEK 32 DAY 4 Daily Language Review

Write the sentences correctly.

1. "Aldo were you think of going to see Fiddler on the Roof on saturday?" asked Lou.

____

2. Aldo replied, "i thought you wanted to go to the hocky game didn't you?"

____

Write the missing word.

3. "Let's decide _______________ to go to the game or the show," Lou said.

   either   whether   neither

What does the underlined phrase mean?

4. "Mom says that my room <u>is a disaster area</u>, so I have to stay and clean it," Aldo said.

____

Read these signal words.

aside from	previously	soon
in spite of	furthermore	therefore
except for	eventually	at last

Which signal word or words best complete each sentence?

1. ________________ President Teddy Roosevelt's reputation as a hunter, he once refused to shoot a bear cub.

2. ________________, that event inspired a cartoon.

3. ________________, the cartoon led a toy manufacturer to create the Teddy Bear.

Write a paragraph using at least three signal words from the box.

4. ____

____

____

____

____

____

WEEK 33 DAY 1 Daily Language Review

Write the sentences correctly.

1. Of all the womans I know Joy is the understandingest.

____

2. When her chickens scattered its food all over their pen Joy didnt complain.

____

Write the word that best completes the sentence. Then explain your choice.

3. Joy's ______________ puppy chewed her tennis shoes to bits.

   evil   wicked   naughty

____

Add punctuation to the sentence.

4. Joy always says, "Theyre just being animals arent they?"

WEEK 33 DAY 2 Daily Language Review

Write the sentences correctly.

1. Throughout History people have send messages in different ways.

____

2. On the battlefield drums trumpets or bagpipes told armys what to do next.

____

Combine the sentences to make one sentence.

3. In the 1800s, new machines were invented. They sent signals through wires.

____

The Greek root *tele* means "far off." What does the bold word in the sentence probably mean?

4. Modern **telecommunications** uses satellites to send data, sound, and pictures.

____

WEEK 33 DAY 3 Daily Language Review

Write the sentences correctly.

1. The loneliest animals is a TV show about animals that are quickly become extinct.

____

2. Creature's like both the great auk or the quagga have die out already.

____

Add punctuation to the sentence.

3. Biologists wildlife centers and the San Diego Dallas and Maryland zoos are trying to keep other rare species alive.

The Latin root *viv* means "live." What does the bold word in the sentence probably mean?

4. Some of their efforts to **revive** rare species have been successful.

____

WEEK 33 DAY 4 Daily Language Review

Write the sentences correctly.

1. Since college Ed had dream of climing the world's higher mountain.

____

2. "Mom and dad someday youl'l see me on top of mount Everest," he stated.

____

Combine the sentences to make one sentence.

3. First he ascended a mountain in New Zealand. Then he wanted more adventure.

____

Write the correct word or words.

4. Edmund Hillary _______________ climbed Everest but also reached the top!

not not only neither

Read these related words and their meanings.

export *verb*
to sell a product in another country

import *verb*
to buy a product from another country

transport *verb*
to move something from one place to another

Which word best completes each sentence?

1. Many countries ____________________ fruits and vegetables from the United States.

2. Japan and China ____________________ parts for electronics to the rest of the world.

3. Barges ____________________ goods through the Bering Strait.

Write a paragraph using all three related words.

4. ____

____

____

____

____

____

WEEK 34 DAY 1 Daily Language Review

Write the sentences correctly.

1. You should give that tree neither more water or more shade Ms. Avery said

____

2. Your rosebush kneads to be pruned, or it doesn't bloom next spring she warned.

____

Use context clues to figure out the meaning of the bold word. Write the meaning on the line.

3. Our **meddlesome** neighbor is always telling us how to take care of our garden.

____

What does the underlined phrase mean?

4. She is <u>as helpful as a rake without teeth</u>.

____

WEEK 34 DAY 2 Daily Language Review

Write the sentences correctly.

1. I just buy the book Bicycle Repair Step by Step, but it looks very helpful.

____

2. After I read the chapter called Stopping Safely I adjust the breaks.

____

Write the missing date.

3. Robin and I are going on a bike ride on ______________.

Monday July 2 Monday, July 2 Monday July, 2

Complete this analogy.

4. finger : hand :: spoke : ______________

WEEK 34 DAY 3 Daily Language Review

Write the sentences correctly.

1. Do you long for piece and quiet because you're home was noisy

2. Were their times when you need to paws in your daily routine and relax

Write the missing word.

3. Visit Shadow Park ____________ you need a break from your busy life.

   until   although   whenever

Explain when you use a conjunction in a sentence.

4. I use a conjunction ____________

WEEK 34 DAY 4 Daily Language Review

Write the sentences correctly.

1. Óbidos is a tiny town in Portugal surrounded by a ancient stone wall

2. Centuries ago a Portuguese king gives the town to his queen as a present

Use context clues to figure out the meaning of the bold word. Write the meaning on the line.

3. You can follow the bike paths that **meander** through the historic neighborhoods.

Complete this analogy.

4. cabin : mansion :: village : ____________

Read the homophones and their meanings.

praise	to give approval or a compliment
prays	says a prayer; wishes very much for something to happen
preys	hunts an animal for food; takes unfair advantage of someone

Which homophone best completes each sentence?

1. The news mentioned a new online scam that ______________ on the elderly.
2. Armando ______________ that his mother's surgery goes well.
3. Our teachers ______________ us when we try hard in class.

Write a paragraph using all three homophones.

4. ____

____

____

____

____

____

WEEK 35 DAY 1 Daily Language Review

Write the sentences correctly.

1. To make your own fossil the first thing to do is, is to put some clay to a paper cup.

____

2. Then you press a object before the clay and careful remove it of the clay.

____

Write the missing word.

3. Next, mix plaster with water and pour it ______________ the cup.

into up between against

Use context clues to figure out the meaning of the bold word. Write the meaning on the line.

4. After the plaster dries, peel off the paper cup and the clay to **reveal** your fossil.

____

WEEK 35 DAY 2 Daily Language Review

Write the sentences correctly.

1. Our class learning a song called Meet Auntie Bellum of Savannah Georgia.

____

2. The song was written from our teacher, whom is write a historical musical.

____

Write the missing word or words.

3. I ______________ tried out for the part of James Oglethorpe.

coulda could have could of

4. I will probably be cast as ______________ Button Gwinnett or James Wright.

neither both either

WEEK 35 DAY 3 Daily Language Review

Write the sentences correctly.

1. Angela was got ready for school where she realized how lately she was.

____

2. "Angela please put away the milk when you have finish," her mother reminded her.

____

Write the missing word.

3. Angela grabbed the milk carton too ______________ and knocked it over.

quick quickly quicker

What does the underlined adage mean?

4. Angela mumbled "<u>haste makes waste</u>" to herself as she cleaned up the spilled milk.

____

WEEK 35 DAY 4 Daily Language Review

Write the sentences correctly.

1. If you'd like a job who helps people in need you might want to be the lifeguard.

____

2. Lifeguards work either seasonal on beaches and all year on city pools.

____

Write the missing word or words.

3. ______________ you already know first aid or not, you must be trained.

Whether Either Not only

4. You ______________ passed a swimming test before you started training.

would of woulda would have

Read these words and their meanings.

lend	to give someone something to use for a short time; to make a loan
defend	to keep someone or something from getting hurt
tame	gentle; well-trained

Circle a word in each sentence that means the *opposite* of the underlined word.

1. I don't want to lend Susie my sweater because she never returned the book that she borrowed last year.

2. The mail carrier used her mailbag to defend herself when the guard dog tried to attack her.

3. Of the two cats we got from the shelter, one still acts wild, but the other is very tame.

Write a paragraph using at least two of the pairs of *opposite* words.

4. ______________________________

____

____

____

____

____

WEEK 36 DAY 1 Daily Language Review

Write the sentences correctly.

1. The tall doorways, that reminded Keon of growing up on the iland of Trinidad.

____

2. "You miss our old Nieghborhood don't you?" his younger sister asked.

____

Write the missing words.

3. "You were just a baby then. Moving ______________ easy for you," he said.

has to be   can be   must have been

Rewrite the sentence to put the words in the best order.

4. Looking at the walking cobblestone narrow paths, he thought of his homeland.

____

WEEK 36 DAY 2 Daily Language Review

Write the sentences correctly.

1. The artical Saving the Wilderness, explains why national parks were created.

____

2. Yellowstone Sequoia and Yosemite being the three national first parks.

____

Write a sentence from this research note.

3. original idea for national parks: George Catlin, artist, 1832

____

The Latin root *migr* means "move to a place." What does the bold word in the sentence probably mean?

4. George Catlin painted pictures of Native Americans during the westward **migration**.

____

WEEK 36 DAY 3 Daily Language Review

Write the sentences correctly.

1. The Dallas Cowboys had to deside both to pass the Ball or run with it.

___

2. When a Seahawks player nocked the ball, it fell, out of the quarterbacks hand.

___

Choose the word that best completes the sentence.

3. There was a ______ to reach the fumbled football.

fight struggle quarrel

Choose the correct word to complete this analogy.

4. basketball : gymnasium :: football : ______

a. touchdown b. player c. stadium

WEEK 36 DAY 4 Daily Language Review

Write the sentences correctly.

1. "I'm never going to be a good Musishan Papa," Chandra complained.

___

2. "Let's find a more pashent clever and helpful Teacher," her father sugested.

___

Rewrite this sentence so it is not a run-on sentence.

3. Chandra's father found an excellent flute teacher her name is Ms. Crawford.

___

What does the underlined phrase mean?

4. Ms. Crawford helped pave the way for Chandra to join the honor band.

___

Read these expressions and their meanings.

clam	a dollar
clam up	to stop talking
happy as a clam	very happy

Which expression best completes each sentence?

1. "Wow! I earned a lot of ____________________!" Emma exclaimed as she saw her first paycheck.

2. When Ali found out the new neighbors had kids his age, he was

   ____________________.

3. I didn't want to take sides in the argument, so I ____________________.

Write a paragraph using all three expressions from the box.

4. ____

My Progress

Week	Number Correct Each Day					Skill I Did Well	Skill I Need to Practice
	1	2	3	4	5		
1							
2							
3							
4							
5							
6							
7							
8							
9							
10							
11							
12							
13							
14							
15							
16							
17							
18							

My Progress (cont.)

Week	Number Correct Each Day					Skill I Did Well	Skill I Need to Practice
	1	2	3	4	5		
19							
20							
21							
22							
23							
24							
25							
26							
27							
28							
29							
30							
31							
32							
33							
34							
35							
36							